UNDERSTANDING THE FOUR MADHHABS

Th[illegible]cts about Ijtihad and Taqlid

Abdal Hakim Murad

Reprinted 2012, 2021

The Muslim Academic Trust
32 London Road
Cambridge CB22 7QH

ISBN 10: 1-902350-01-4
ISBN 13: 978-1-902350-01-1

DESIGNED BY ABD AL-LATEEF WHITEMAN

Printed in Turkey by Mega Printing

بسم الله الرحمن الرحيم

Understanding the Four Madhhabs

THE UMMA'S greatest achievement over the past millenium has undoubtedly been its internal intellectual cohesion. From the fifth century of the Hijra almost to the present day, and despite the outward drama of the clash of dynasties, the Sunni Muslims have maintained an almost unfailing attitude of religious respect and brotherhood among themselves. It is a striking fact that virtually no religious wars, riots or persecutions divided them during this extended period, so difficult in other ways.

The history of religious movements suggests that this is an unusual outcome. The normal sociological view, as expounded by Max Weber and his disciples, is that religions enjoy an initial period of unity, and then descend into an increasingly bitter factionalism led by rival hierarchies. Christianity has furnished the most obvious example of this; but one could add many others, including secular faiths such as Marxism. On the face of it, Islam's ability to avoid this fate is astonishing, and demands careful analysis.

There is, of course, a straightforwardly religious explanation. Islam is the final religion, the 'last bus home', and as such has been divinely secured from the more terminal forms of decay. It is true that what Abdul Wadod Shalabi has termed 'spiritual entropy'[1] has been at work ever since Islam's inauguration, a fact which is well-supported by a number of hadiths. Nonetheless, Providence has not neglected the Umma. Earlier religions slide gently or painfully into schism and irrelevance; but Islamic piety, while fading in quality, has been given mechanisms which allow it to retain much of the sense of unity emphasised in its glory days. Wherever the antics of the emirs and politicians might lead, the brotherhood of believers, a reality in the initial career of Christianity and some other faiths, continues, fourteen hundred years on, to be a compelling principle for members of the final and definitive community of revelation in Islam. The reason is simple and unarguable: God has given us this religion as His last word, and it must therefore endure, with its essentials of *tawḥīd*, worship and ethics intact, until the Last Days.

Such an explanation has obvious merit. But we will still need to explain some painful exceptions to the rule in the earliest phase of our history. The Prophet himself ﷺ had told his Companions, in a hadith narrated by Imām Tirmidhī, that 'Whoever among you outlives me shall see a vast dispute.' The initial schisms: the disastrous revolt against ʿUthmān ؓ,[2] the clash between ʿAlī ؓ and Ṭalḥa, and then with Muʿāwiya,[3] the bloody scissions of the Khārijites[4] — all these drove knives of discord into the Muslim body politic almost from the outset. Only the inherent sanity and love of unity among scholars of the Umma — assisted, no doubt, by Providence — overcame the early spasms of factionalism, and created a strong and harmonious Sunnism which has, at least on the purely religious plane, united ninety percent of the Umma for ninety percent of its history.[5]

It will help us greatly to understand our modern, increasingly divided situation if we look closely at those forces which divided us in the distant past. There were many of these, some of them very eccentric; but only two took the form of mass popular movements, driven by religious ideology, and in active rebellion against majoritarian faith and scholarship. For good reasons, these two acquired the names of Khārijism and Shīʿism. Unlike Sunnī Islam, both were highly productive of splinter groups and sub-movements; but they nonetheless remained as recognisable traditions of dissidence because of their ability to express the two great divergences from mainstream opinion on the key question of the source of religious authority in Islam.

Confronted with what they saw as moral slippage among early caliphs, posthumous partisans of ʿAlī ؓ developed a theory of religious authority which departed from the older egalitarian assumptions by vesting it in a charismatic succession of Imāms. We need not stop here to investigate the question of whether this idea was influenced by the Eastern Christian background of some early converts, who had been nourished on the idea of the mystical apostolic succession to Christ, a gift which supposedly gave the Church the unique ability to read his mind for later generations. What needs to be appreciated is that Shīʿism, in its myriad forms, developed as a response to a widely-sensed lack of definitive religious authority in early Islamic society. As the age of the Righteous Caliphs came to a close, and the Umayyad rulers departed ever more conspicuously from the lifestyle expected of them as 'Commanders of the

Faithful', the sharply-divergent and still nascent schools of *fiqh* seemed inadequate as sources of strong and unambiguous authority in religious matters. Hence the often irresistible seductiveness of the idea of an infallible Imām.[6]

This interpretation of the rise of Imāmism also helps to explain the second great phase in Shīʿī expansion. After the success of the fifth-century Sunnī Revival, when Sunnism seemed at last to have become a fully coherent system, Shīʿism went into a slow eclipse. Its extreme wing, as manifested in Ismāʿīlism, received a heavy blow at the hands of Imām al-Ghazālī, whose book *Scandals of the Bāṭinites* exposed and refuted their secret doctrines with devastating force.[7] This decline in Shīʿī fortunes was only arrested after the mid-seventh century, once the Mongol hordes under Genghis Khān had invaded and obliterated the central lands of Islam. The onslaught was unimaginably harsh: we are told, for instance, that out of a hundred thousand former inhabitants of the city of Herāt, only forty survivors crept out of the smoking ruins to survey the devastation. In the wake of this tidal wave of mayhem, newly-converted Turcoman nomads moved in, who, with the Sunnī ulema of the cities dead, and a general atmosphere of fear, turbulence, and Messianic expectation in the air, turned readily to extremist forms of Shīʿī belief.[9] The triumph of Shīʿism in Iran, a country once loyal to Sunnism, dates back to that painful period.[10]

The other great dissident movement in early Islam was that of the Khārijites, literally, the 'seceders', so-called because they seceded from the army of the Caliph ʿAlī ﵁ when he agreed to settle his dispute with Muʿāwiya through arbitration. Calling out the Koranic slogan, 'Judgement is only God's', they fought bitterly against ʿAlī and his army which included many of the leading Companions, until, in the year 38, Imām ʿAlī defeated them at the Battle of Nahrawān, where some ten thousand of them perished.[11]

Although the first Khārijites were destroyed, Khārijism itself lived on. As it formulated itself, it turned into the precise opposite of Shīʿism, rejecting any notion of inherited or charismatic leadership, and stressing that leadership of the community of believers should be decided by piety alone. This was assessed by very rudimentary criteria: the early Khārijites were known for extreme toughness in their devotions, and for the harsh doctrine that any Muslim who commits a major sin is an unbeliever. This notion of *Takfīr* (declaring Muslims to be outside Islam), permitted the Khārijite groups, camping out in remote mountain districts of Khūzestān, to raid Muslim settlements which had accepted Umayyad authority. Non-Khārijīs were routinely slaughtered in these operations, which brought merciless reprisals from tough Umayyad generals such as al-Ḥajjāj ibn Yūsuf. But despite the apparent hopelessness of their cause, the Khārijite attacks continued. The Caliph ʿAlī ﷺ was assassinated by Ibn Muljam, a survivor of Nahrawān, while the Ḥadīth scholar Imām al-Nasā'ī, author of one of the most respected collections of *sunan*, was likewise murdered by Khārijite fanatics in Damascus in 303/915.[12]

Like Shīʿism, Khārijism caused much instability in Iraq and Central Asia, and on occasion elsewhere, until the fourth and fifth centuries of Islam. At that point, something of historic moment occurred. Sunnism managed to unite itself into a detailed system that was now so well worked-out, and so obviously the way of the great majority of ulema, that the attraction of the rival movements diminished sharply.

What happened was this. Sunnī Islam, occupying the middle ground between the two extremes of egalitarian Khārijism and hierarchical Shīʿism, had long been preoccupied with disputes over its own concept of authority. For the Sunnīs, authority was, by definition, vested in the Koran and Sunna. But confronted with the enormous body of hadiths, which had been scattered in various forms and narrations throughout the length and breadth of the Islamic world following the migrations of the Companions and Followers, the Sunna sometimes posed serious problems of interpretation. Even when the sound hadiths had been sifted out from this great body of material, which totalled several hundred thousand hadith reports, there were some hadiths which appeared to conflict with each other, or even with verses of the Koran. It was obvious that simplistic approaches such as that of the Khārijites, namely, establishing a small corpus of hadiths and deriving doctrines and law from them directly, were not going to work. The apparent internal contradictions were too numerous, and the interpretations placed on them too complex, for the *qāḍīs* to be able to dish out judgements simply by opening the Koran and hadith collections to an appropriate page.

The reasons underlying cases of apparent conflict between various revealed texts were scrutinised closely by the early ulema, often amid sustained debate between brilliant minds armed with the most perfect photographic memories. Much of the science of Islamic jurisprudence (*uṣūl al-fiqh*) was developed in order to provide consistent mechanisms for resolving such conflicts in a way which ensured fidelity to the basic ethos of Islam. The term *taʿāruḍ al-adilla* ('mutual contradiction of proof-texts') is familiar to all students of Islamic jurisprudence as one of the most sensitive and complex of all Muslim legal concepts.[13] Early scholars such as Ibn Qutayba felt obliged to devote whole books to the subject.[14]

The ulema of *uṣūl* recognised as their starting assumption that conflicts between the revealed texts were no more than conflicts of interpretation, and could not reflect inconsistencies in the Lawgiver's message as conveyed by the Prophet ﷺ. The message of Islam had been perfectly conveyed before his demise; and the function of subsequent scholars was exclusively one of interpretation, not of amendment.

Armed with this awareness, the Islamic scholar, when examining problematic texts, begins by attempting a series of preliminary academic tests and methods of resolution. The system developed by the early ulema was that if two Koranic or hadith texts appeared to contradict each other, then the scholar must first analyse the texts linguistically, to see if the contradiction arises from an error in interpreting the Arabic. If the contradiction cannot be resolved by this method, then he must attempt to determine, on the basis of a range of textual, legal and historiographic techniques, whether one of them is subject to *takhṣīṣ*, that is, concerns special circumstances only, and hence forms a specific exception to the more general principle enunciated in the other text.[15] The jurist must also assess the textual status of the reports, recalling the principle that a Koranic verse will overrule a Hadith related by only one *isnād* (the type of hadith known as *āḥād*), as will a hadith supplied by many *isnāds* (*mutawātir* or *mashhūr*).[16] If, after applying all these mechanisms, the jurist finds that the conflict remains, he must then investigate the possibility that one of the texts was subject to formal abrogation (*naskh*) by the other.

This principle of *naskh* is an example of how, when dealing with the delicate matter of *taʿāruḍ al-adilla*, the Sunnī ulema founded their approach on textual policies which had already been recognised many times during the lifetime of the Prophet ﷺ. The Companions knew by *ijmāʿ* that over the years of the Prophet's ministry, as he taught and nurtured them, and brought them from the wildness of paganism to the sober and compassionate path of monotheism, his teaching had been divinely shaped to keep pace with their development. The best-known instance of this was the progressive prohibition of wine, which had been discouraged by an early Koranic verse, then condemned, and finally prohibited.[17] Another example, touching an even more basic principle, was the canonical prayer, which the early Umma had been obliged to say only twice daily, but which, following the Miʿrāj, was increased to five times a day.[18] *Mutʿa* (temporary marriage) had been permitted in the early days of Islam, but was subsequently prohibited as social conditions developed, respect for women grew, and morals became firmer.[19] There are several other instances of this, most being datable to the years immediately following the Hijra, when the circumstances of the young Umma changed in radical ways.

There are two types of *naskh*: explicit (*ṣarīḥ*) or implicit (*ḍimnī*).[20] The former is easily identified, for it involves texts which themselves specify that an earlier ruling is being changed. For instance, there is the verse in the Koran (2:144) which commands the Muslims to turn in prayer to the Holy Kaᶜba rather than to Jerusalem.[21] In the hadith literature this is even more frequently encountered; for example, in a hadith narrated by Imām Muslim we read: 'I used to forbid you to visit graves; but you should now visit them.'[22] Commenting on this, the ulema of hadith explain that in early Islam, when idolatrous practices were still fresh in people's memories, visiting graves had been forbidden because of the fear that some new Muslims might commit *shirk* there. As the Muslims grew stronger in their monotheism, however, this prohibition was discarded as no longer necessary, so that today it is a recommended practice for Muslims to go out to visit graves in order to pray for the dead and to be reminded of the *ākhira*.[23]

The other type of *naskh* is more subtle, and often taxed the brilliance of the early Ulema to the limit. It involves texts which cancel earlier ones, or modify them substantially, but without actually stating that this has taken place. The ulema have given many examples of this, including the two verses in Sūrat al-Baqara which give differing instructions as to the period for which widows should be maintained out of an estate (2:240 and 234).[24] And in the hadith literature, there is the example of the incident in which the Prophet ﷺ once told the Companions that when he prayed sitting because he was burdened by some illness, they should sit behind him. This hadith is given by Imām Muslim. And yet we find another hadith, also narrated by Muslim, which records an incident in which the Companions prayed standing while the Prophet ﷺ was sitting. The apparent contradiction has been resolved by careful chronological analysis, which shows that the latter incident took place after the former, and therefore takes precedence over it.[25]

The techniques of *naskh* identification have enabled the ulema to resolve most of the recognised cases of *taᶜāruḍ al-adilla*. They demand a rigorous and detailed knowledge not just of the hadith disciplines, but of history, *sīra*, and of the views held by the Companions and other scholars on the circumstances surrounding the genesis and exegesis of the hadith in question. In some cases, hadith scholars would travel throughout the Islamic world to locate the required information pertinent to a single hadith.[26]

In cases where in spite of all efforts, abrogation cannot be proven, then the ulema of the *salaf* recognised the need to apply further tests. Important among these is the analysis of the *matn* (the transmitted text rather than the *isnād* of the hadith).[27] 'Clear' (*ṣarīḥ*) statements are deemed to take precedence over 'allusive' ones (*kināya*), and 'definite' (*muḥkam*) words take precedence over words falling into more ambiguous categories, such as the 'interpreted' (*mufassar*), the 'obscure' (*khafī*) and the 'problematic' (*mushkil*).[28] It may also be necessary to look at the position of the narrators of the conflicting hadiths, giving precedence to the report issuing from the individual who was more directly involved. A famous example of this is the hadith narrated by Maymūna which states that the Prophet ﷺ married her when not in a state of consecration (*iḥrām*) for the pilgrimage. Because her report was that of an eyewitness, her hadith is given precedence over the conflicting report from Ibn ʿAbbās, related by a similarly sound *isnād*, which states that the Prophet was in fact in a state of *iḥrām* at the time.[29]

There are many other rules, such as that which states that 'prohibition takes precedence over permissibility'.[30] Similarly, conflicting hadiths may be resolved by utilising the *fatwā* of a Companion, after taking care that all the relevant *fatwās* are compared and assessed.[31] Finally, recourse may be had to *qiyās* (analogy).[32] An example of this is the various reports about the solar eclipse prayer (*ṣalāt al-kusūf*), which specify different numbers of bowings and prostrations. The ulema, having investigated the reports meticulously, and having been unable to resolve the contradiction by any of the mechanisms outlined above, have applied analogical reasoning by concluding that since the prayer in question is still called '*ṣalāt*', then the usual form of *ṣalāt* should be followed, namely, one bowing and two prostrations. The other hadiths are to be abandoned.[33]

This careful articulation of the methods of resolving conflicting source-texts, so vital to the accurate derivation of the *sharīʿa* from the revealed sources, was primarily the work of Imām al-Shāfiʿī. Confronted by the confusion and disagreement among the jurists of his day, and determined to lay down a consistent methodology which would enable a *fiqh* to be established in which the possibility of error was excluded as far as was humanly possible, Shāfiʿī wrote his brilliant *Risāla* (*'Treatise on Islamic Jurisprudence'*). His ideas were soon taken up, in varying ways, by jurists of the other major traditions of law; and today they are fundamental to the formal application of the *sharīʿa*.[34]

Shāfiʿī's system of minimising mistakes in the derivation of Islamic rulings from the mass of evidence came to be known as *uṣūl al-fiqh* (the 'roots of *fiqh*'). Like the other formal academic disciplines of Islam, this was not an innovation in the negative sense, but a working-out of principles already discernible in the time of the earliest Muslims. In time, each of the great interpretative traditions of Sunnī Islam codified its own variation on these 'roots' (*uṣūl*), thereby yielding in some cases divergent 'branches' (*furūʿ*, i.e. specific rulings on practice). Although the debates generated by these divergences could sometimes be energetic, nonetheless, they were insignificant when compared to the great sectarian and legal disagreements which had arisen during the first two centuries of Islam before the science of *uṣūl al-fiqh* had put a stop to such chaotic discord.

It hardly needs remarking that although the Four Imāms, Abū Ḥanīfa, Mālik ibn Anas, al-Shāfiʿī and Ibn Ḥanbal, are regarded as the founders of these four great traditions, which, if we were asked to define them, we might sum up as 'sophisticated techniques for avoiding innovation', their traditions were fully systematised only by later generations of scholars. The Sunni ulema rapidly recognised the brilliance of the Four Imāms, and after the late third century of Islam we find that hardly any scholars adhered to any other school. The great hadith specialists were all loyal adherents of one or another of the *madhhabs*, particularly that of Imām al-Shāfiʿī. But within each *madhhab*, leading scholars continued to improve and refine the 'roots' and 'branches' of their school. In some cases, historical conditions made this not only possible, but necessary. For instance, scholars of the school of Imām Abū Ḥanīfa, which was built on the foundations of the early legal schools of Kūfa and Baṣra, were wary of some hadiths in circulation in Iraq because of the prevalence of forgery engendered by the strong sectarian influences there. Later, however, once the canonical collections of Bukhārī, Muslim and others became available, subsequent generations of Ḥanafī scholars took the entire corpus of hadiths into account in formulating and revising their *madhhab*. This type of process continued for two centuries, until the Schools reached a condition of maturity in the fourth and fifth centuries of the Hijra.[35]

It was at that time, too, that the attitude of toleration and good opinion between the Schools became universally accepted. This was formulated by Imām al-Ghazālī, himself the author of four textbooks of Shāfiʿī *fiqh*,[36] and also of *al-Mustaṣfā*, widely acclaimed as the most advanced and careful of all works on *uṣūl al-fiqh*. With his well-known concern for sincerity, and his dislike of ostentatious scholarly rivalry, he strongly condemned what he called 'fanatical attachment to a *madhhab*'.[37] While it was necessary for the Muslim to follow a recognised *madhhab* in order to avert the lethal danger of misinterpreting the revealed sources, he must never fall into the trap of considering his own school categorically superior to the others. With a few insignificant exceptions in the late Ottoman period, the great scholars of Sunnī Islam have followed the ethos outlined by Imām al-Ghazālī, and have been conspicuously respectful of each others' *madhhab*. Anyone who has studied under the gracious and open-minded ulema of traditional Islam will be well-aware of this fact.[38]

The evolution of the Four Schools did not stifle, as some Orientalists have suggested,[39] the capacity for the refinement or extension of positive law.[40] On the contrary, sophisticated mechanisms were available which not only permitted qualified individuals to derive the *sharīʿa* from the Koran and Sunna on their own authority, but actually obliged them to do this. According to most scholars, an expert who has fully mastered the sources and fulfilled a variety of necessary scholarly conditions is not permitted to follow the prevalent rulings of his School, but must derive the rulings himself from the revealed sources. Such an individual is known as a *mujtahid*,[41] a term derived from the well-known hadith of Muʿādh ibn Jabal.[42]

Few would seriously deny that for a Muslim to venture beyond established expert opinion and have recourse directly to the Qur'an and Sunna, he must be a scholar of great eminence. The danger of people misunderstanding the sources and hence damaging the *Sharīʿa* is a very real one, as was shown by the discord and strife which afflicted some early Muslims in the period which preceded the establishment of the Orthodox Schools. Prior to Islam, entire religions had been subverted by inadequate scriptural scholarship, and it was vital that Islam should be secured from a comparable fate.

In order to protect the *Sharīʿa* from the danger of innovation and distortion, the great scholars of *uṣūl* laid down rigorous conditions which must be fulfilled by anyone wishing to claim the right of *ijtihād* for himself.[43] These conditions include: (a) mastery of the Arabic language, to minimise the possibility of misinterpreting Revelation on purely linguistic grounds; (b) a profound knowledge of the Koran and Sunna and the circumstances surrounding the revelation of each verse and hadith, together with a full knowledge of the Koranic and hadith commentaries, and a control of all the interpretative techniques discussed above; (c) knowledge of the specialised disciplines of hadith, such as the assessment of narrators and of the *matn*; (d) knowledge of the views of the Companions, Followers and the great Imāms, and of the positions and reasoning expounded in the textbooks of *fiqh*, combined with the knowledge of cases where a consensus (*ijmāʿ*) has been reached; (e) knowledge of the science of juridical analogy (*qiyās*), its types and conditions; (f) knowledge of one's own society and of the public interest (*maṣlaḥa*); (g) knowing the general objectives (*maqāṣid*) of the Sharīʿa; (h) a high degree of intelligence and personal piety, combined with the Islamic virtues of compassion, courtesy, and modesty.

A scholar who has fulfilled these conditions can be considered a *mujtahid fi'l-sharʿ*, and is not obliged, or even permitted, to follow an existing authoritative *madhhab*.[44] This is what some of the Imāms were saying when they forbade their great disciples from imitating them uncritically. But for the much greater number of scholars whose expertise has not reached such dizzying heights, it may be possible to become a *mujtahid fi'l-madhhab*, that is, a scholar who remains broadly convinced of the doctrines of his school, but is qualified to differ from received opinion within it.[45] There have been a number of examples of such men, for instance Qāḍī Ibn ʿAbd al-Barr among the Mālikīs, Imām al-Nawawī among the Shāfiʿīs, Ibn ʿĀbidīn among the Ḥanafīs, and Ibn Qudāma among the Ḥanbalīs. All of these scholars considered themselves followers of the fundamental interpretative principles of their own *madhhabs*, but are on record as having exercised their own gifts of scholarship and judgement in reaching many new verdicts within them.[46] It is to these experts that the Mujtahid Imāms directed their advice concerning *ijtihād*, such as Imām al-Shāfiʿī's instruction that 'if you find a hadith that contradicts my verdict, then follow the hadith.'[47] It is obvious that whatever some writers nowadays like to believe, such counsels were intended for the Imām's sophisticated pupils, and were never intended for use by the Islamically-uneducated masses. Imām al-Shāfiʿī was not addressing a crowd of butchers, nightwatchmen and donkey-drovers.

Other categories of *mujtahids* are listed by the *uṣūl* scholars; but the distinctions between them are subtle and not relevant to our theme.[48] The remaining categories can in practice be reduced to two: the *muttabiʿ* ('follower'), who follows his *madhhab* while being aware of the Koranic and hadith texts and the reasoning underlying its positions,[49] and secondly the *muqallid* ('emulator'), who simply conforms to the *madhhab* because of his confidence in its scholars, and without necessarily knowing the detailed reasoning behind all its thousands of rulings.[50]

Clearly it is recommended for the *muqallid* to learn as much as he or she is able of the formal proofs of the *madhhab*. But it is equally clear that not every Muslim can be a scholar. Scholarship takes a lot of time, and for the Umma to function properly most people must have other employment: as accountants, soldiers, butchers, and so forth.[51] As such, they cannot reasonably be expected to become great ulema as well, even if we suppose that all of them have the requisite intelligence. The Holy Koran itself states that less well-informed believers should have recourse to qualified experts: 'So ask the people of remembrance, if you do not know' (16:43).[52] (According to the scholars, the 'people of remembrance' are the ulema.) And in another verse, the Muslims are enjoined to create and maintain a group of specialists who provide authoritative guidance for non-specialists: 'A band from each community should stay behind to gain instruction in religion and to warn the people when they return to them, so that they may take heed' (9:122). Given the depth of scholarship needed to understand the revealed texts accurately, and the extreme warnings we have been given against distorting the Revelation, it is obvious that ordinary Muslims are duty bound to follow expert opinion, rather than rely on their own reasoning and limited knowledge. This obvious duty was well-known to the early Muslims: the *khalīfa* ʿUmar ﵁ followed certain rulings of Abū Bakr ﵁, saying 'I would be ashamed before God to differ from the view of Abū Bakr'. And Ibn Masʿūd ﵁, in turn, despite being a *mujtahid* in the fullest sense, used in certain issues to follow ʿUmar ﵁. According to al-Shaʿbī: 'Six of the Companions of the Prophet ﷺ used to give *fatwās* to the people: Ibn Masʿūd, ʿUmar ibn al-Khaṭṭāb, ʿAlī, Zayd ibn Thābit, Ubayy ibn Kaʿb, and Abū Mūsā (al-Ashʿarī). And out of these, three would abandon their own judgements in favour of the judgements of three others: ʿAbdallāh (ibn Masʿūd) would abandon his own judgement for the judgement of ʿUmar, Abū Mūsā would abandon his own judgement for the judgement of ʿAlī, and Zayd would abandon his own judgement for the judgement of Ubayy ibn Kaʿb.'[53]

This verdict, namely that one is well-advised to rely on a great Imām as one's guide to the Sunna, rather than relying on oneself, is particularly binding upon Muslims in countries such as Britain, among whom only a small percentage is even entitled to have a choice in this matter. This is for the simple reason that unless one knows Arabic,[54] then even if one wishes to read all the hadith determining a particular issue, one cannot. For various reasons, including their great length, no more than ten of the basic hadith collections have been translated into English. There remain well over three hundred others, including such seminal works as the *Musnad* of Imām Aḥmad ibn Ḥanbal,[55] the *Muṣannaf* of Ibn Abī

Shayba,[56] the *Ṣaḥīḥ* of Ibn Khuzayma,[57] the *Mustadrak* of al-Ḥākim,[58] and many other multi-volume collections, which contain large numbers of sound hadiths which cannot be found in Bukhārī, Muslim, or the other works that have so far been translated. Even if we assume that the existing translations are entirely accurate, it is obvious that a policy of trying to derive the *Sharīʿa* directly from the Book and the Sunna cannot be attempted by those who have no access to the Arabic. To attempt to discern the *Sharīʿa* merely on the basis of the hadiths which have been translated will be to ignore and amputate much of the *sunna*, leading to serious distortions.[59]

Let me give just two examples of this. The Sunnī *Madhhabs*, in their rules for the conduct of legal cases, lay down the principle that the canonical punishments (*ḥudūd*) should not be applied in cases where there is the least ambiguity, and that the *qāḍī* should actively strive to prove that such ambiguities exist. An amateur reading in the Sound Six collections will find no certain confirmation of this.[60] But the *madhhab* ruling is based on a hadith recorded in the *Muṣannaf* of Ibn Abī Shayba, the *Musnad* of al-Ḥārithī, and the *Musnad* of Musaddad ibn Musarhad. The text is: 'Ward off the *ḥudūd* by means of ambiguities'.[61] Imām al-Ṣanʿānī, in his book *Al-Ansāb*, narrates the circumstances of this hadith: 'A man was found drunk, and was brought to ʿUmar, who ordered the *ḥadd* of eighty lashes to be applied. When this had been done, the man said: "ʿUmar, you have wronged me! I am a slave!' (Slaves receive only half the punishment.) ʿUmar was grief-stricken at this, and recited the Prophetic hadith, 'Ward off the *ḥudūd* by means of ambiguities."'[62]

Another example is provided by the practice of *istighfār* for others during the Ḥajj. According to a hadith, 'Forgiveness is granted to the Ḥajjī, and to those for whom the Ḥajjī prays.' This hadith is not related in any of the collections so far translated into English; but it is narrated, by a sound *isnād*, in many other collections, including *al-Muʿjam al-Ṣaghīr* of al-Ṭabarānī and the *Musnad* of al-Bazzār.[63]

Because of the traditional pious fear of distorting the Law of Islam, the overwhelming majority of the great scholars of the past — certainly well over ninety-nine percent of them — have adhered loyally to a *madhhab*.[64] It is true that in the troubled fourteenth century a handful of dissenters appeared, such as Ibn Taymiya and Ibn al-Qayyim;[65] but even these individuals never recommended that semi-educated Muslims should attempt *ijtihād* without expert help. And in any case, although these authors have recently been resurrected and made prominent, their influence on the orthodox scholarship of classical Islam was negligible, as is suggested by the small number of manuscripts of their works preserved in the great libraries of the Islamic world.[66]

Nonetheless, social turbulences have in the past century thrown up a number of writers who have advocated the abandonment of authoritative scholarship. The most prominent figures in this campaign were Muḥammad ᶜAbduh and his disciple Muḥammad Rashīd Riḍā.[67] Dazzled and intimidated by the triumph of the West, these men urged Muslims to throw off "the shackles of *taqlīd*", and to reject the authority of the Four Schools. Today in some Arab capitals, especially where the indigenous tradition of orthodox scholarship has been weakened, it is common to see young Arabs filling their homes with every hadith collection they can lay their hands upon, and poring over them in the apparent belief that they are less likely to misinterpret this vast and complex literature than Imām al-Shāfiᶜī, Imām Aḥmad, and the other great Imāms. This irresponsible approach, now increasingly widespread, is predictably opening the door to sharply divergent opinions, which have seriously damaged the unity, credibility and effectiveness of the Islamic movement, and provoked sharp arguments over issues settled by the great Imāms over a thousand years ago.[68] It is common now to see activists prowling the mosques, criticising other worshippers for what they believe to be defects in their worship, even when their victims are following the verdicts of some of the leading Imāms of *fiqh*. The unpleasant, Pharisaic atmosphere generated by this activity has the effect of discouraging many less committed Muslims from attending the mosque at all. No-one now recalls the view of the early ulema, which was that Muslims should tolerate divergent interpretations of the Sunna as long as these interpretations have been held by reputable scholars. As Sufyān al-Thawrī said: 'If you see a man doing something over which there is a debate among the scholars, and which you yourself believe to be forbidden, you should not forbid him from doing it.'[69] The alternative to this policy is, of course, a disunity and rancour which will poison the Muslim community from within.[70]

In a Western-influenced global culture in which people are urged from early childhood to 'think for themselves' and to challenge established authority, it can sometimes be difficult to muster enough humility to recognise one's own limitations.[71] We are all a little like Pharaoh: our egos are by nature resistant to the idea that anyone else might be much more intelligent or learned than ourselves. The belief that ordinary Muslims, even if they know no Arabic, are qualified to derive rulings of the *Sharīᶜa* for themselves, is an example of this egotism running wild.

To young people proud of their own judgement, and unfamiliar with the complexity of the sources and the brilliance of authentic scholarship, this 'do-it-yourself' type of religion can be an effective trap, which ends by luring them away from the orthodox path of Islam and into an unintentional agenda of provoking deep divisions among the Muslims. The fact that all the great scholars of the religion, including the hadith experts, themselves belonged to *madhhabs*, and required their students to belong to *madhhabs*, seems to have been forgotten. Self-esteem has won a major victory here over common sense and Islamic responsibility.[72]

The Holy Koran commands Muslims to use their minds and reflective capacities; and the issue of following qualified scholarship is an area in which this faculty must be very carefully deployed. The basic point should be appreciated that no categoric difference exists between *uṣūl al-fiqh* and any other specialised science requiring lengthy training. Shaykh Sa'īd Ramaḍān al-Būṭī, who has articulated the orthodox response to the anti-*Madhhab* trend in his book: *Non-Madhhabism: The Greatest Bidʿa Threatening the Islamic Sharīʿa*, likes to compare the science of deriving rulings to that of medicine. If one's child is seriously ill, he asks, does one look for oneself in the medical textbooks for the proper diagnosis and cure, or should one go to a trained medical practitioner? Clearly, sanity dictates the latter option. And so it is in matters of religion, which are in reality even more important and potentially hazardous: we would be both foolish and irresponsible to try to look through the sources ourselves, and become our own *muftīs*. Instead, we should recognise that those who have spent their entire lives studying the Sunna and the principles of law are far less likely to be mistaken than we are.[73]

Another metaphor might be added to this, this time borrowed from astronomy. We might compare the Koranic verses and the hadiths to the stars. With the naked eye, we are unable to see many of them clearly; so we need a telescope. If we are foolish, or proud, we may try to build one ourselves. If we are sensible and modest, however, we will be happy to use one built for us by Imām Mālik or Ibn Ḥanbal, and refined, polished and improved by generations of great astronomers. A *madhhab* is, after all, nothing more than a piece of precision equipment enabling us to see Islam with the maximum clarity possible. If we use our own devices, our amateurish efforts will inevitably distort our vision.

A third image might also be deployed. An ancient building, for instance the Blue Mosque in Istanbul, might seem imperfect to some who worship in it.

Young enthusiasts, burning with a desire to make the building still more exquisite and well-made (and no doubt more in conformity with their own time-bound preferences), might gain access to the crypts and basements which lie under the structure, and, on the basis of their own understanding of the principles of architecture, try to adjust the foundations and pillars which support the great edifice above them. They will not, of course, bother to consult professional architects, except perhaps one or two whose rhetoric pleases them — nor will they be guided by the books and memoirs of those who have maintained the structure over the centuries. Their zeal and pride leaves them with no time for that. Groping through the basements, they bring out their picks and drills, and set to work with a blind enthusiasm.

There is a real danger that Sunni Islam is being treated in a similar fashion. The edifice has stood for centuries, withstanding the most bitter blows of its enemies. Only from within can it be weakened. No doubt, Islam has intelligent foes among whom this fact is well-known. The spectacle of the disunity and *fitnas* which divided the early Muslims despite their superior piety, and the solidity and cohesiveness of Sunnism after the final codification of the *Sharīʿa* in the four Schools of the great Imāms, must have put ideas into many a malevolent head. This is not to suggest in any way that those who attack the great *Madhhabs* are the conscious tools of Islam's enemies. But it may go some way to explaining why they will continue to be well-publicised and well-funded, while the orthodox alternative is starved of resources. With every Muslim now a proud *Mujtahid*, and with *taqlīd* dismissed as a sin rather than a humble and necessary virtue, the divergent views which caused such pain in our early history will surely break surface again. Instead of four *madhhabs* in harmony, we will have a billion *madhhabs* in bitter and self-righteous conflict. No more brilliant scheme for the destruction of Islam could ever have been devised.[74]

NOTES

1 Abdul Wadod Shalabi, *Islam: Religion of Life* (2nd ed., Dorton, 1989), 10. This is the purport of the famous hadith: 'The best generation is my own, then that which follows them, then that which follows them'. (Muslim, Faḍā'il al-Ṣaḥāba, 210, 211, 212, 214.)

2 The Khalīfa was killed by Muslim rebels from Egypt, whose grievances included his alleged 'innovation' of introducing a standard text of the Holy Koran. (Evidently the belief among some modern Muslims that there can be no such thing as a 'good innovation' (*bidʿa ḥasana*) has a long history!) For the full story, see pages 63-71 of M.A. Shaban, *Islamic History AD 600-750 (AH 132): A New Interpretation* (Cambridge, 1971).

3 Shaban, 73-7.

4 For the Khārijites see Imām al-Ṭabarī, *History*, vol.XVIII, translated by M. Morony (New York, 1987), 21-31. Their monstrous joy at having assassinated the khalīfa ʿAlī ibn Abī Ṭālib is recorded on page 22.

5 For an account of the historical development of the *fiqh*, see Ahmad Hasan, *The Early Development of Islamic Jurisprudence* (Islamabad, 1970); Hilmi Ziyâ Ülken, *Islam Düşüncesi* (Istanbul, 1946), 68-100; Ömer Nasûhî Bilmen, *Hukuki Islamiyye ve Istilahatı Fikhiyye Kamusu* (Istanbul, 1949-52), I, 311-338.

6 For a brief account of Shīʿism, see C. Glassé, *The Concise Encyclopedia of Islam* (London, 1989), 364-70.

7 *Faḍā'iḥ al-Bāṭinīya*, ed. ʿAbd al-Raḥmān Badawī (Cairo, 1964).

8 For a detailed but highly readable account of the Mongol onslaught see B. Spuler, *History of the Mongols, based on Eastern and Western Accounts of the Thirteenth and Fourteenth Centuries* (London, 1972); the best-known account by a Muslim historian is ʿAlā' al-Dīn al-Juwaynī, *Tārīkh-i Jihāngushā*, translated by J.A. Boyle as *The History of the World-Conqueror* (Manchester, 1958).

9 For the slaughter of the ulema, see the dramatic account of Aḥmad Aflākī, *Manāqib al-ʿĀrifīn*, ed. Tahsin Yazıcı (Ankara, 1959-61), I, 21, who states that 50,000 scholars were killed in the city of Balkh alone.

10 The critical battle was fought in 873/1469, when the Mongol ruler of Iran was defeated by the Turkomans of the (Sunnī) Ak Koyunlu dynasty, who were in turn defeated by Shāh Ismāʿīl, an extreme Shīʿite, in 906-7/1501, who inaugurated the Safavid rule which turned Iran into a Shīʿī country. (*The Cambridge History of Iran*, VI, 174-5; 189-350; Sayyid Muḥammad Sabzavarī, tr. Sayyid Ḥasan Amīn, *Islamic Political and Juridical Thought in Safavid Iran* [Tehran, 1989].)

11 The Khārijites represent a tendency which has reappeared in some circles in recent years. Divided into many factions, their principles were never fully codified. They were

textualist, puritanical and anti-intellectual, rejected the condition of Quraishite birth for their Imām, and declared everyone outside their grouping to be *kāfir*. For some interesting accounts, see M. Kafafi, 'The Rise of Khārijism', *Bulletin of the Faculty of Arts of the University of Egypt*, XIV (1952), 29-48; Ibn Ḥazm, *al-Fiṣal fi'l-milal wa'l-niḥal* (Cairo, 1320), IV, 188-92; Brahim Zerouki, *L'Imāmat de Tahart: premier etat musulman du Maghreb* (Paris, 1987).

12 Probably because he had written a book celebrating the virtues of the caliph ᶜAlī. See Ibn Ḥajar al-ᶜAsqalānī, *Tahdhīb al-Tahdhīb* (Hyderabad, 1325), I, 36-40.

13 See, for example, Imām al-Ḥaramayn al-Juwaynī, *al-Burhān fi uṣūl al-fiqh* (Cairo, 1400), §§1189-1252.

14 Ibn Qutayba, *Ta'wīl Mukhtalif al-Ḥadīth* (Cairo, 1326). Readers of French will benefit from the translation of G. Lecomte: *Le Traité des divergences du hadith d'Ibn Qutayba* (Damascus, 1962). There is also a useful study by Ishaq al-Husayni: *The Life and Works of Ibn Qutayba* (Beirut, 1950). Mention should also be made of a later and in most respects similar work, by Imām al-Ṭaḥāwī (d.321): *Mushkil al-Āthār* (Hyderabad, 1333), which is more widely used among the ulema.

15 Imām Abu'l-Walīd al-Bājī (d.474), *Iḥkām al-Fuṣūl ilā ᶜIlm al-Uṣūl*, ed. A. Turkī (Beirut, 1986/1407), §§184-207; Imām Abū Isḥāq al-Shirāzī (d.476), *al-Lumaᶜ fī uṣūl al-fiqh* (Cairo, 1377), 17-24; Juwaynī, §§327-52, 1247; Imām al-Shāfiᶜī, tr. Majid Khadduri, *Al-Shāfiᶜī's Risāla: Treatise on the Foundations of Islamic Jurisprudence* (Cambridge, 1987), 103-8. Shāfiᶜī gives a number of well-known examples of Koranic texts being subject to *takhṣīṣ*. For instance, the verse '*As for the thief, male and female, cut off their hands as a retribution from Allah,*' (5:42) appears to be unconditional; however it is subject to *takhṣīṣ* by the hadith which reads 'Hands should not be cut off for fruits, nor the spadix of a palm tree, and that the hand should not be cut off unless the price of the thing stolen is a quarter of a dinar or more.' (Mālik, *Muwaṭṭa'*, Abū Daūd, *Sunan*; see Shāfiᶜī, *Risāla*, 105.)

16 Mohammad Hashim Kamali, *Principles of Islamic Jurisprudence* (Cambridge, 1991), 356-65. This excellent book by a prominent Afghan scholar is by far the best summary of the theory of Islamic law, and should be required reading for every Muslim who wishes to raise questions concerning the *Sharīᶜa* disciplines.

17 The verses in question were: 2:219, 4:43, and 5:93. See Kamali, 16-17.

18 Kamali, 150; Ibn Rushd, *The Distinguished Jurist's Primer*, tr. Imran Nyazee and Muhammad Abdul Rauf (Reading, 1994), 97. This new translation of the great classic *Bidāyat al-Mujtahid*, is a fascinating explanation of the basic arguments over the proof-texts (*adilla*) used by the scholars of the recognised *madhhabs*. Ibn Rushd was a Mālikī *qāḍī*, but presents the views of other scholars with the usual respect and objectivity. The work is the best-known example of a book of the *Sharīᶜa* science of *ᶜilm al-khilāf* (the 'Knowledge of Variant Rulings'; for a definition of this science see Imām Ḥujjat al-Islām al-Ghazālī, *al-Mustaṣfā min ᶜilm al-uṣūl*, [Cairo, 1324] I, 5).

19 Kamali, 150 quoting Shāṭibī, *Muwāfaqāt*, III, 63.

20 Kamali, 154-160; Bājī, §§383-450; Shirāzī, 30-5; Juwaynī, §§1412-1454; Ghazālī, *Mustaṣfā*, I, 107-129. The problem was first addressed systematically by Imām al-Shāfiʿī. 'There are certain hadiths which agree with one another, and others which are contradictory to one another; the abrogating and the abrogated hadiths are clearly distinguished [in some of them]; in others the hadiths which are abrogating and abrogated are not indicated.' (*Risāla*, 179.) For cases in which the Holy Koran has abrogated a hadith, or (more rarely) a hadith has abrogated a Koranic verse, see Ghazālī, *Mustaṣfā*, I, 124-6; Bājī, §429-39; Juwaynī, §1440-3. The *sunna* is able to abrogate the Koran because it too is a revelation (*waḥy*); as Imām al-Bājī explains it, 'The Blessed Prophet's own *sunna*s do not in reality abrogate anything themselves; they only state that Allah has cancelled the ruling of a Koranic passage. Hence the abrogation, in reality, is from Allah, whether the abrogating passage is in the Koran or the *Sunna*.' (Bājī, §435.)

21 For this as an instance of abrogation, see Shāfiʿī, *Risāla* (Khadduri), 133.

22 Muslim, Janā'iz, 100.

23 Kamali, 154.

24 Kamali, 155; see also Shāfiʿī, *Risāla* (Khadduri), 168.

25 Sayf ad-Din Ahmed Ibn Muhammad, *Al-Albani Unveiled: An Exposition of His Errors and Other Important Issues* (London, 2nd ed., 1415), 49-51; Ibn Rushd, *The Distinguished Jurist's Primer*, 168-170; Shāfiʿī, *Risāla* (Khadduri), 199-202.

26 M.Z. Siddiqi, *Ḥadīth Literature, its Origins, Development and Special Features* (Revised ed. Cambridge, 1993), 3, 40, 126.

27 Defects in the *matn* can sometimes make a hadith weak even if its *isnād* is sound (Siddiqi, 113-6).

28 Kamali, 361; Bilmen, I, 74-6, 82-4. The classification of revealed texts under these headings is one of the most sensitive areas of *uṣūl al-fiqh*.

29 Kamali, 361.

30 Kamali, 362.

31 Kamali, 235-44; Ghazālī, *Mustaṣfā*, 1, 191-2; Juwaynī, §343.

32 For some expositions of the difficult topic of *qiyās*, see Kamali, 197-228; Shirāzī, 53-63; Juwaynī, §§676-95; Imām Sayf al-Dīn al-Āmidī (*al-Iḥkām fī Uṣūl al-Aḥkām*, Cairo, 1332/1914), III, 261-437, IV, 1-161.

33 Kamali, 363-4.

34 The accessible English translation of his best-known work on legal theory has already been mentioned above in note 15.

35 The question is often asked why only four schools should be followed today. The answer is straightforward: while in theory there is no reason whatsoever why the number has to be four, the historical fact is that only these four have sufficient detailed literature to support them. In connection with the hyper-literalist Ẓāhirī *madhhab*, Ibn Khaldūn

writes: 'Worthless persons occasionally feel obliged to follow the Ẓāhirī school and study these books in the desire to learn the Ẓāhirī system of jurisprudence from them, but they get nowhere, and encounter the opposition and disapproval of the great mass of Muslims. In doing so they often are considered innovators, as they accept knowledge from books for which no key is provided by teachers.' (*Muqaddima*, tr. F. Rosenthal [Princeton, 1958], III, 6.)

36 These are (in order of length, shortest first), *al-Khulāṣa, al-Wajīz, al-Wasīṭ and al-Basīṭ*. The great Imām penned over a hundred other books, earning him from a grateful Umma the title 'Ḥujjat al-Islām' (The Proof of Islam). It is hardly surprising that when the ulema quote the famous *ṣaḥīḥ* hadith 'Allah shall raise up for this Umma at the beginning of each century someone who will renew for it its religion,' they cite Imām al-Ghazālī as the renewer of the fifth century of Islam. See for instance Imām Muḥammad al-Sakhāwī (d.902AH), *al-Maqāṣid al-Ḥasana fī bayān kathīrin min al-aḥādīth al-mushtahira ʿalā al-alsina* (Beirut, 1405), 203-4, who lists the 'renewers' as follows: ʿUmar ibn ʿAbd al-ʿAzīz, al-Shāfiʿī, Ibn Surayj, Abū Ḥāmid al-Isfarāīnī, Ḥujjat al-Islām al-Ghazālī, Fakhr al-Dīn al-Rāzī, Ibn Daqīq al-ʿĪd, al-Balqīnī. Imām Ibn ʿAsākir (d.571 AH), in his famous work *Tabyīn Kadhib al-Muftarī fīmā nusiba ilā al-Imām Abi'l-Ḥasan al-Ashʿarī*, ed. Imām Muhammad Zāhid al-Kawtharī (Damascus, 1347, reproduced Beirut, 1404), 52-4, has the following list: ʿUmar ibn ʿAbd al-ʿAzīz, al-Shāfiʿī, al-Ashʿarī, al-Bāqillānī, al-Ghazālī.

37 Imām Abū Ḥāmid al-Ghazālī, *Iḥyā' ʿUlūm al-Dīn* (Cairo: Muṣṭafā al-Ḥalabī, 1347), III, 65.

38 'The most characteristic qualities of the great ulema are dignity and serenity, respect for other scholars, compassionate concern for the Umma, and following the Prophet, upon whom be blessings and peace, whose view was always broad, his wisdom perfect, and his toleration superb.' Imām Yūsuf al-Dajawī (d. 1365 AH), *Maqālāt wa-Fatāwā* (Cairo: Majmaʿ al-Buḥūth al-Islāmīya, 1402), II, 583. 'True fairness is to regard all the Imāms as worthy; whoever follows the *madhhab* of a Mujtahid because he has not attained the degree of *Ijtihād*, is not harmed by the fact that other *imāms* differ from his own.' (Shāṭibī, *Iʿtiṣām*, III, 260.) There are many examples cited by the scholars to show the respect of the *madhhabs* for each other. For instance, Shaykh Ibrāhīm al-Samadī (d.1662), a pious scholar of Damascus, once prayed to be given four sons, so that each might follow one of the recognised *madhhabs*, thereby bringing a fourfold blessing to his house. (Muḥammad al-Amīn al-Muḥibbī, *Khulāṣat al-athar fī aʿyān al-qarn al-ḥādī ʿashar* [Cairo, 1248], I, 48.) And it was not uncommon for scholars to be able to give *fatwās* in more than one *madhhab* (such a man was known technically as *muftī al-firaq*). (Ibn al-Qalanīsī, *Dhayl Tārīkh Dimashq* [Beirut, 1908], 311.) Hostility between the *Madhhabs* was rare, despite some abuse in the late Ottoman period. Al-Dhahabī counsels his readers as follows: 'Do not think that your own *madhhab* is the best, and the one most beloved by Allah, for you have no proof of this. The Imāms, may Allah be pleased with them, all follow great

goodness; when they are right, they receive two rewards, and when they are wrong, they still receive one reward.' (al-Dhahabī, *Zaghal al-ᶜIlm wa'l-Ṭalab*, 15, quoted in Saᶜīd Ramaḍān al-Būṭī, *Al-Lāmadhhabīya Akhṭar Bidᶜa tuhaddid al-Sharīᶜa al-Islāmīya*, 3rd edition, Beirut 1404, 81.) The final words here ('right ... reward') are taken from a well-known hadith to this effect (Bukhārī, *Iᶜtiṣām*, 21).

39 Most notoriously N. Coulson, *Conflicts and Tensions in Islamic Jurisprudence* (Chicago, 1969), 43, 50, 96; but also I. Goldziher, Louis Gardet and Montgomery Watt.

40 It will be useful here to refute an accusation made by some Orientalists, and even by some modern Muslims, who suggest that the scholars were reluctant to challenge the *madhhab* system because if they did so they would be 'out of a job', and lucrative *qāḍī* positions, restricted to followers of the orthodox Schools, would be barred to them. This is a particularly distasteful example of the modern tendency to slander men whose moral integrity was no less impressive than their learning: to suggest that the great Ulema of Islam followed the interpretation of Islam that they did simply for financial reasons is insulting and a disgraceful form of *ghība* (backbiting). In any case, it can be easily refuted. The great ulema of the past were in almost every case men of independent means, and did not need to earn from their scholarship. For instance, Imām Ibn Ḥajar had inherited a fortune from his mother (al-Sakhāwī, *al-Ḍaw' al-Lāmiᶜ li-Ahl al-Qarn al-Tāsiᶜ* [Cairo, 1353-5], II, 36-40). Imām al-Suyūṭī came from a prominent and wealthy family of civil servants (see his own *Ḥusn al-Muḥāḍara fī akhbār Miṣr wa'l-Qāhira* [Cairo, 1321], I, 153, 203). For examples of scholars who achieved financial independence see the editor's notes to Ibn Jamāᶜa's *Tadhkirat al-Sāmiᶜ fī Ādāb al-ᶜĀlim wa'l-Mutaᶜallim* (Hyderabad, 1353), 210: Imām al-Bājī was a craftsman who made gold leaf: 'his academic associates recall that he used to go out to see them with his hand sore from the effects of the hammer' (Dhahabī, *Tadhkira*, III, 349-50); while the great Khalīl ibn Isḥāq, also a Mālikī, was a soldier who had taken part in the liberation of Alexandria from the Crusaders, and often gave his fiqh classes while still wearing his chain mail and helmet (Suyūṭī, *Ḥusn al-Muḥāḍara*, I, 217.) And it was typical for the great scholars to live lives of great frugality: Imām al-Nawawī, who died at the age of 44, is said to have damaged his health by his ascetic lifestyle: for instance, he declined to eat of the fruit of Damascus, where he taught, because it was grown on land whose legal status he regarded as suspect. (al-Yāfiᶜī, *Mir'āt al-Janān wa-ᶜIbrat al-Yaqẓān* [Hyderabad, 1338], IV, 185.) It is not easy to see how such men could have allowed motives of financial gain to dictate their approach to religion.

41 A *mujtahid* is a scholar qualified to perform *ijtihād*, defined as 'personal effort to derive a Sharīᶜa ruling of the *furūᶜ* from the revealed sources.' (Bilmen, I, 247.) His chief task — the actual process of derivation — is called *istinbāṭ*, originally signifying in Arabic 'bringing up water with difficulty from a well.' (Bilmen, I, 247.)

42 'When Allah's Messenger, upon him be blessings and peace, wished to send Muᶜādh ibn Jabal to the Yemen, he asked him: 'How will you judge if an issue is presented to you

for judgement?' 'By what is in Allah's Book', he replied. 'And if you do not find it in Allah's Book?' 'Then by the *Sunna* of Allah's Messenger.' 'And if it is not in the *Sunna* of Allah's Messenger?' 'Then I shall strive in my own judgement' (*ajtahidu ra'yī*). (Abū Dāūd, Aqḍiya, 11.)

43 Kamali, 366-393, especially 374-7; see also Āmidī, IV, 219-11; Shirāzī, 71-2; Bilmen, I, 247, 250, 251-2.

44 Kamali, 386-8. Examples of such men from the time of the Tābiᶜūn onwards include 'Ibrāhīm al-Nakhaᶜī, Ibn Abī Layla, Ibn Shubruma, Sufyān al-Thawrī, al-Ḥasan ibn Ṣāliḥ, al-Awzāᶜī, ᶜAmr ibn al-Ḥārith, al-Layth ibn Saᶜd, ᶜAbdallāh ibn Abī Jaᶜfar, Isḥāq ibn Rāhawayh, Abū ᶜUbayd al-Qāsim ibn Salām, Abū Thawr, Ibn Khuzayma, Ibn Naṣr al-Marwazī, Ibn Mundhir, Daūd al-Ẓāhirī, and Ibn Jarīr al-Ṭabarī, may Allah show them all His mercy.' (Bilmen, I, 324.) It should be noted that according to some scholars a concession (*rukhṣa*) exists on the matter of the permissibility of *taqlīd* for a *mujtahid*: Imām al-Bājī and Imām al-Ḥaramayn, for instance, permit a *mujtahid* to follow another *mujtahid* in cases where his own research to establish a matter would result in dangerous delay to the performance of a religious duty. (Bājī, §783; Juwaynī, §1505.)

45 Kamali, 388; Bilmen, I, 248.

46 'The major followers of the great Imāms did not simply imitate them as some have claimed. We know, for instance, that Abū Yūsuf and al-Shaybānī frequently dissented from the position of Abū Ḥanīfa. In fact, it is hard to find a single question of *fiqh* which is not surrounded by a debate, in which the independent reasoning and *ijtihād* of the scholars, and their determination to locate the precise truth, are very conspicuous. In this way we find Imām al-Shāfiᶜī determining, in his new *madhhab*, that the time for Maghrib does not extend into the late twilight (*shafaq*); while his followers departed from this position in order to follow a different proof-text (*dalīl*). Similarly, Ibn ᶜAbd al-Barr and Abū Bakr ibn al-ᶜArabī hold many divergent views in the *madhhab* of Imām Mālik. And so on.' (Imām al-Dajawī, II, 584.)

47 'Whenever a *mujtahid* reaches a judgement in which he goes against *ijmāᶜ*, or the basic principles, or an unambiguous text, or a clear *qiyās* (*al-qiyās al-jalī*) free of any proof which contradicts it, his *muqallid* is not permitted to convey his view to the people or to give a *fatwā* in accordance with it ... however no-one can know whether this has occurred who has not mastered the principles of jurisprudence, clear *qiyās*, unambiguous texts, and anything that could intervene in these things; and to know this one is obliged to learn *uṣūl al-fiqh* and immerse oneself in the ocean of *fiqh*.' (Imām Shihāb al-Dīn al-Qarāfī, *al-Furūq* (Cairo, 1346), II, 109.)

48 The ulema usually recognise seven different degrees of Muslims from the point of view of their learning, and for those who are interested they are listed here, in order of scholarly status. (1, 2) The *mujtahidūn fi'l-sharᶜ* (*Mujtahids* in the *Sharīᶜa*) and the *mujtahidūn fi'l-madhhab* (*Mujtahids* in the *Madhhab*) have already been mentioned. (3)

Mujtahidūn fi'l-masā'il (*Mujtahids* on Particular Issues) are scholars who remain within a school, but are competent to exercise ijtihād on certain aspects within it which they know thoroughly. (4) *Aṣḥāb al-Takhrīj* (Resolvers of Ambiguity), who are competent to 'indicate which view was preferable in cases of ambiguity, or regarding suitability to prevailing conditions'. (5) *Aṣḥāb al-Tarjīḥ* (People of Assessment) are 'those competent to make comparisons and distinguish the correct (*ṣaḥīḥ*) and the preferred (*rājiḥ, arjaḥ*) and the agreed-upon (*muftā bihā*) views from the weak ones' inside the *madhhab*. (6) *Aṣḥāb al-Taṣḥīḥ* (People of Correction): 'those who could distinguish between the manifest (*ẓāhir al-riwāya*) and the rare and obscure (*nawādir*) views of the schools of their following.' (7) *Muqallidūn*: the 'emulators', including all non-scholars. (Kamali, 387-9. See also Bilmen, I, 250-1, 324-6.) Of these seven categories, only the first three are considered to be *mujtahids*.

49 This is explained by Imām al-Shāṭibī in the context of the following passsage, all of which is quoted here to furnish a further summary of the orthodox position on *taqlīd*. 'A person obliged to follow the rules of the *Sharīᶜa* must fall into one of three categories. [I] He may be a *mujtahid*, in which case, he will practise the legal conclusions to which his *ijtihād* leads him. [II] He may be a complete *muqallid*, unappraised of the knowledge required. In his case, he must have a guide to lead him, and an arbitrator to give judgements for him, and a scholar to emulate. Obviously, he follows the guide only in his capacity as a man possessed of the requisite knowledge. The proof for this is that if he knows, or even suspects, that he does not in fact possess it, it is not permissible for him to follow him or to accept his judgement; in fact, no individual, whether educated or not, should think of following through *taqlīd* someone whom he knows is not qualified, in the way that a sick man should not put himself in the hands of someone whom he knows is not a doctor. [III] He may not have attained to the level of the *Mujtahids*, but he understands the *dalīl* and its context, and is competent to understand it in order to prefer some rulings over others in certain questions. In his case, one must either recognise his preferences and views, or not. If they are recognised, then he becomes like a *mujtahid* on that issue; if they are not, then he must be classed along with other ordinary non-specialist Muslims, who are obliged to follow Mujtahids. (*al-Iᶜtiṣām* [Cairo, 1913-4] III, 251-3.)

An equivalent explanation of the status of the *muttabiᶜ* is given by Āmidī, IV, 306-7: 'If a non-scholar, not qualified to make *ijtihād*, has acquired some of the knowledge required for *ijtihād*, he must follow the verdicts of the *Mujtahids*. This is the view of the correct scholars, although it has been rejected by some of the Muᶜtazilites in Baghdad, who state: "That is not allowable, unless he obtains a clear proof (*dalīl*) of the correctness of the *ijtihād* he is following." But the correct view is that which we have stated, this being proved by the Koran, *Ijmāᶜ* and the intellect. The Koranic proof is Allah's statement, "Ask the people of remembrance if you do not know," which is a general (*ᶜāmm*) commandment to all. The proof by *Ijmāᶜ* is that ordinary Muslims in the time of the

Companions and the Followers used to ask the *mujtahids*, and follow them in their *Sharī*ʿ*a* judgements, while the learned among them would answer their questions without indicating the *dalīl*. They would not forbid them from doing this, and this therefore constitutes *Ijmā*ʿ on the absolute permissibility of an ordinary Muslim following the rulings of a *mujtahid*.' For Āmidī's intellectual proof, see note 51 below.

50 A *muqallid* is a Muslim who practises *taqlīd*, which is the *Sharī*ʿ*a* term for 'the acceptance by an ordinary person of the judgement of a *muftī*.' (Juwaynī, §1545.) The word '*muftī*' here means either a *mujtahid* or someone who authentically transmits the verdict of a *mujtahid*. 'As for the ordinary person [ʿ*āmmī*], it is obligatory [*wājib*] upon him to make *taqlīd* of the *ulema*.' (Bājī, §783.) The actual choice of which *mujtahid* an ordinary Muslim should follow is clearly a major responsibility. 'A *muqallid* may only make *taqlīd* of another person after carefully examining his credentials, and obtaining reliable third-party testimony as to his scholarly attainments' (Juwaynī, §1511). (Imām Ibn Fūrak, however, holds that a *mujtahid's* own self-testimony is sufficient.) Imām Juwaynī goes on to observe (§1515) that it is necessary to follow the best *mujtahid* available; which is also the position of Imām al-Bājī (§794). See also Shirāzī (p.72): 'It is not permissible for someone asking for a *fatwā* to ask just anyone, lest he ask someone who has no knowledge of the *fiqh*. Instead, it is obligatory (*wājib*) for him to ascertain the scholar's learning and trustworthiness.' And Qarāfī (II, 110): 'The *Salaf*, may Allah be pleased with them, were intensely reluctant to give *fatwās*. Imām Mālik said, "A scholar should not give *fatwās* until he is regarded as competent to do so both by himself and by others." In other words, the scholars must be satisfied of his qualifications. Imām Mālik did not begin to give *fatwās* until he had been given permission (*ijāza*) to do so by forty turbaned ones [scholars].'

51 'The *dalīl* for our position is Allah's commandment: So ask the people of remembrance, if you do not know. For if we forbade *taqlīd*, everyone would need to become an advanced scholar, and no-one would be able [have time] to earn anything, and the earth would lie uncultivated.' (Shirāzī, 71.) 'The intellectual proof [of the need for *taqlīd*] is that if an issue of the *furū*ʿ arises for someone who does not possess the qualifications for *ijtihād* then he will either not adopt an Islamic ruling at all, and this is a violation of *Ijmā*ʿ, or, alternatively, he will adopt an Islamic ruling, either by investigating the proofs involved, or by *taqlīd*. But an adequate investigation of the proofs is not possible for him, for it would oblige him, and all humanity, fully to investigate the *dalīls* pertaining to the issues, thereby distracting them from their sources of income, and leading to the extinction of crafts and the ruin of the world.' (Āmidī, *Iḥkām*, IV, 307-8.) 'One of the *dalīls* for the legitimacy of following the verdicts of the scholars is our knowledge that anyone who looks into these discussions and seeks to deduce rulings of *Sharī*ʿ*a* will need to have the right tools, namely, the science of the rulings of the Koran and Sunna and *uṣūl al-fiqh*, the principles of rhetoric and the Arabic language, and other sciences which are not easily acquired, and which most people cannot attain to. And even if some of them do attain to

it, they only do so after long study, investigation and very great effort, which would require that they devote themselves entirely to this and do nothing else; and if ordinary people were under the obligation to do this, there would be no cultivation, commerce, or other employments which are essential for the continuance of humanity — and it is the *ijmāʿ* of the Umma that this is something which Allah *taʿālā* has not obliged His slaves to do. ... There is therefore no alternative for them to following the ulema.' (Bājī, §793.)

52 'There is *ijmāʿ* among the scholars that this verse is a commandment to whoever does not know a ruling or the *dalīl* for it to follow someone who does. Almost all scholars of *uṣūl al-fiqh* have made this verse their principal *dalīl* that it is obligatory for an ordinary person to follow a scholar who is a *mujtahid*.' (al-Būṭī, 71; translated also in Keller, 17.)

53 See also Dajawī, II, 576: 'The Companions and Followers used to give *fatwās* on legal issues to those who asked for them. At times they would mention the source, if this was necessary, while at other times they would limit themselves to specifying the ruling.' Al-Ghazālī (*Mustaṣfā*, II, 385) explains that the existence of *taqlīd* and *fatwā* among the Companions is a *dalīl* for the necessity of this fundamental distinction: 'The proof that *taqlīd* is obligatory is the *ijmāʿ* of the Companions. For they used to give *fatwās* to the ordinary people and did not command them to acquire the degree of *ijtihād* for themselves. This is known necessarily (*bi'l-ḍarūra*) and by parallel lines of transmission (*tawātur*) from both the scholars and the non-scholars among them.' See also Ibn Khaldūn, *Muqaddima* (Būlāq ed., p.216): 'Not all the Companions were qualified to give *fatwās*, and Islam was not taken from all of them. That privilege was held only by those who had learnt the Koran, knew what it contained by way of abrogated and abrogating passages, ambiguous (*mutashābih*) and perspicuous (*muḥkam*) expressions, and its other special features.' And also Imām al-Bājī (§793): 'Ordinary Muslims have no alternative but to follow the Ulema. One proof of this is the *ijmāʿ* of the Companions, for those among them who had not attained the degree of *ijtihād* used to ask the ulema of the Companions for the correct ruling on something which happened to them. Not one of the Companions criticised them for so doing; on the contrary, they gave them *fatwās* on the issues they had asked about, without condemning them or telling them to derive the rulings themselves [from the Koran and Sunna].' See also Imām al-Āmidī in note 49 above.

A list of the *muftīs* among the Companions is given by Juwaynī (§§1494-9); they include the Four Khalīfas, Ṭalḥa ibn ʿUbaydillāh, ʿAbd al-Raḥmān ibn ʿAwf, and Saʿd ibn Abī Waqqāṣ. Others were not *muftīs*, such as Abū Hurayra, who despite his many narrations of hadiths was never known for his judgements (§1497). Shirāzī (p.52) confirms the obvious point that some Companions are considered more worthy of being followed in legal matters than others.

54 As we have seen above, the ulema regard a mastery of the Arabic language as one of the essential qualifications for deriving the *Sharīʿa* directly from the Koran and Sunna. See

Juwaynī, §§70-216, where this is stressed. Juwaynī records that Imām al-Shāfiʿī was so expert in the Arabic language, grammar and rhetoric that at a very young age he was consulted by the great philologist al-Asmaʿī, who asked his help in editing some early and very difficult collections of Arabic poetry. (Juwaynī, §1501.) We also learn that Imām 'Ibn al-Mubārak, the famous traditionist of Merv, spent more money on learning Arabic than on traditions [hadith], attaching more importance to the former than the latter, and asking the students of hadith to spend twice as long on Arabic than on hadith ... Al-Asmaʿī held that someone who studied hadith without learning grammar was to be categorised with the forgers of hadith.' (Siddiqi, 84-5.)

55 Published in 6 volumes in Cairo in 1313 AH. Another work by him, the *Kitāb al-Zuhd* (Beirut, 1403), also contains many hadiths.

56 Published in 13 volumes in Bombay between 1386 and 1390.

57 Edited by M.M. al-Aʿẓamī, Beirut, 1391-97.

58 This is an important collection of hadiths whose accuracy Imām al-Ḥākim al-Nīsābūrī considered to meet the criteria of Imāms al-Bukhārī and Muslim, but which had not been included in their collections. Published in four large volumes in Hyderabad between 1334 and 1342.

59 Needless to say, the amateurs who deny *taqlīd* and try to derive the rulings for themselves are even more ignorant of the derivative sources of *Sharīʿa* than they are of the Koran and Sunna. These other sources do not only include the famous ones such as *ijmāʿ* and *qiyās*. For instance, the *fatwās* of the Companions are considered by the ulema to be a further important source of legislation. 'Imām al-Shāfiʿī throughout his life taught that *diya* (bloodmoney) was increased in cases of crimes committed in the Ḥaramayn or the Sacred Months, and he had no basis for this other than the statements of the Companions.' (Juwaynī, §1001.)

60 There is a version of this hadith in Tirmidhī (Ḥudūd, 2), but attached to an *isnād* which includes Yazīd ibn Ziyād, who is weak.

61 Ibn Abī Shayba, *Muṣannaf*, XI, 70.

62 Sakhāwī, 74-5.

63 Sakhāwī, 742.

64 For a complete list of the most famous scholars of Islam and the *madhhabs* to which they belonged see Sayf ad-Din Ahmad, *Al-Albani Unveiled*, 97-9.

65 For these writers see Aḥmad ibn al-Naqīb al-Miṣrī, tr. Nuh Keller, *Reliance of the Traveller* (Abu Dhabi, 1991), 1059-60, 1057-9. The attitude of Ibn al-Qayyim is not consistent on this issue. In some passages of his *Iʿlām al-Muwaqqiʿīn* he seems to suggest that any Muslim is qualified to derive rulings directly from the Koran and Sunna. But in other passages he takes a more intelligent view. For instance, he writes: 'Is it permissible for a *muftī* who adheres to the *madhhab* of his Imām to give a *fatwā* in accordance with a different *madhhab* if that is more correct in his view? [The answer is] if he is [simply]

following the principles of that Imām in procedures of *ijtihād* and ascertaining the proof-texts [i.e. is a *mujtahid fi'l-madhhab*], then he is permitted to follow the view of another *mujtahid* which he considers correct.' (*Iʿlām al-Muwaqqiʿīn*, IV, 237.) This is a broad approach, but is nonetheless very far from the notion of simply following the '*dalīl*' every time rather than following a qualified interpreter. This quote and several others are given by Shaykh al-Būṭī to show the various opinions held by Ibn al-Qayyim on this issue, which, according to the Shaykh, reveal 'remarkable contradictions'. (Al-Būṭī, 56-60.)

66 Many of Ibn Taymiya's works exist only as single manuscripts; and even the others, when compared to the works of the great scholars such as al-Suyūṭī and al-Nawawī, seem to have been copied only very rarely. See the list of ancient manuscripts of his works given by C. Brockelmann, *Geschichte der arabischen Litteratur* (2nd. ed. Leiden, 1943-9), II, 126-7, Supplement, II, 119-126.

67 ʿAbduh, in turn, was influenced by his teacher and collaborator Jamāl al-Dīn al-Afghānī (1839-97). Afghānī was associated with that transitional 'Young Ottoman' generation which created the likes of Namık Kemāl and (somewhat later) Zia Gökalp and Sāṭiʿ al-Ḥuṣarī: men deeply traumatised by the success of the Western powers and the spectacle of Ottoman military failure, and who sought a cultural renewal by jettisoning historic Muslim culture while maintaining authenticity by retaining a 'pristine essence'. In this they were inspired, consciously or otherwise, by the wider 19th century quest for authenticity: the nationalist philosophers Herder and Le Bon, who had outlined a similar revivalist-essentialist project for France and Germany based on the 'original sources' of their national cultures, had been translated and were widely read in the Muslim world at the time. Afghānī was not a profound thinker, but his pamphlets and articles in the journal which he and ʿAbduh edited, *al-ʿUrwat al-Wuthqā*, were highly influential. Whether he believed in his own pan-Islamic ideology, or indeed in his attenuated and anti-historicist version of Islam, is unclear. When writing in contexts far from his Muslim readership he often showed an extreme scepticism. For instance, in his debate with Renan concerning the decline of Arab civilisation, he wrote of Islam: 'It is clear that wherever it becomes established, this religion tried to stifle the sciences and it was marvellously served in its designs by despotism.' (Reply to Renan, translated by N. Keddie in *An Islamic Response to Imperialism: Political and Religious Writings of Sayyid Jamal al-Din 'al-Afghani'* (Berkeley and Los Angeles, 1968), 183, 187. It is hardly surprising that ʿAbduh should have worked hard to suppress the Arabic translation of this work!

Afghānī's reformist ideology led him to found a national political party in Egypt, al-Ḥizb al-Waṭanī, including not only Muslims, but in which 'all Christians and Jews who lived in the land of Egypt were eligible for membership.' (Jamal Ahmed, *The Intellectual Origins of Egyptian Nationalism* (London, 1960), 16.) This departure from traditional Islamic notions of Muslim solidarity can be seen as a product of Afghānī's specific attitude to *taqlīd*. But his pupil's own *fatwās* were often far more radical, perhaps because of

ʿAbduh's 'partiality for the British authority which pursued similar lines of reform and gave him support' (Ahmed, 35). We are not surprised to learn that the British governor of Egypt, Lord Cromer, wrote: 'For many years I gave to Mohammed Abdu all the encouragement in my power' (Lord Cromer, *Modern Egypt* [New York, 1908], II, 180). An example is the declaration in ʿAbduh's *tafsīr* (much of which is by Riḍā) that the erection of statues is *ḥalāl*. The same argument was being invoked by Atatürk, who, when asked why he was erecting a statue of himself in Ankara, claimed that 'the making of statues is not forbidden today as it was in the days when Muslims were just out of idolatry, and that it is necessary for the Turks to practise this art, for it is one of the arts of civilization'. (C. Adams, *Islam and Modernism in Egypt* [London, 1933], 193-4.)

68 A poorly-argued but well-financed example of a book in this category is a short text by the Saudi-based Uzbek writer al-Khujandī, of which an amended version exists in English. This text aroused considerable concern among the ulema when it first appeared in the 1960s, and Shaykh Saʿīd Ramaḍān al-Būṭī's book was in fact written specifically in refutation of it. The second and subsequent editions of al-Būṭī's work, which shows how Khujandī systematically misquoted and distorted the texts, contain a preface which includes an account of a meeting between al-Būṭī and the Albanian writer Nāṣir al-Dīn al-Albānī (d.1420/1999), who was associated with Khujandī's ideas. The three-hour meeting, which was taped, was curious inasmuch as al-Albānī denied that Khujandī was stating that all Muslims can derive rulings directly from the Koran and Sunna. For instance, where Khujandī makes the apparently misleading statement that 'As for the *Madhhabs*, these are the views and *ijtihāds* of the ulema on certain issues; and neither Allah nor His messenger have compelled anyone to follow them,' al-Albānī explains that 'anyone' (*aḥad*) here in fact refers to 'anyone qualified to make *ijtihād*'. (Al-Būṭī, 13.) Al-Albānī went on to cite several other instances of how readers had unfortunately misunderstood Khujandī's intention. Shaykh al-Būṭī, quite reasonably, replied to the Albanian writer: 'No scholar would ever use language in such a loose way and make such generalisations, and intend to say something so different to what he actually and clearly says; in fact, no-one would understand his words in the way that you have interpreted them.' Albānī's response was: 'The man was of Uzbek origin, and his Arabic was that of a foreigner, so he was not able to make himself as clear as an Arab would. He is dead now, and we should give him the benefit of the doubt and impose the best interpretation we can on his words!' (al-Būṭī, 14.) But al-Albānī, despite his protestations, is reliably said to have persisted in his belief that *taqlīd* is unacceptable. *Wa-lā ḥawla wa-lā quwwata illā bi'Llāh.*

69 The ulema also quote the following guiding principle of Islamic jurisprudence: 'That which is wrong (*munkar*) need not be condemned as [objectively] wrong unless all scholars agree (in *ijmāʿ*) that it is so.' (Dajawī, II, 583.) Imām al-Dajawī (II, 575) also makes the following points: 'The differences of opinion among the ulema are a great mercy

(*raḥma*) upon this Umma. ᶜUmar ibn ᶜAbd al-ᶜAzīz declared: "It would not please me if the Companions of Muḥammad, upon whom be blessings and peace, had not disagreed, for had they not done so, no mercy would have come down." Yaḥyā ibn Saᶜīd, one of the great hadith narrators among the Followers (*Tābiᶜūn*), said: "The people of knowledge are a people of broadness (*ahl tawsiᶜa*). They continue to give *fatwās* which are different from each other, and no scholar reproaches another scholar for his opinion." However, if ordinary people took their rulings straight from the Koran and Sunna, as a certain faction desires, their opinions would be far more discordant than this, and the Four Schools would no longer be four, but thousands. Should that day come, it will bring disaster upon disaster for the Muslims — may we never live to see it!'

One could add that 'that day' seems already to be upon us, and that the resulting widening of the argument on even the most simple juridical matters is no longer tempered by the erstwhile principles of politeness and toleration. The fiercely insulting debate between Nāṣir al-Dīn al-Albānī and the Saudi writer Ḥammūd al-Tuwayjirī is a typical instance. The former writer, in his book *Ḥijāb al-Mar'a al-Muslima*, uses the Koran and Sunna to defend the view that a woman may expose her face in public; while the latter, in his *al-Ṣārim al-Mashhūr ᶜalā Ahl al-Tabarruj wa'l-Sufūr*, attacks Albānī in the most vituperative terms for failing to draw from the revealed sources the supposedly obvious conclusion that women must always veil their faces from non-*maḥram* men. Other examples of the bitter hatred generated by the non-*Madhhab* style of discord, based in attempts at direct *istinbāṭ*, are unfortunately many. Hardly any mosque or Islamic organisation nowadays seems to be free of them.

The solution is to recall the principle referred to above, namely that two *mujtahids* can hold differing opinions on the *furūᶜ*, and still be rewarded by Allah, while both opinions will constitute legitimate *fiqh*. (Juwaynī, §§1455-8; Bilmen, I, 249.) This is clearly indicated in the Koranic verses: 'And Daūd and Sulaymān, when they gave judgement concerning the field, when people's sheep had strayed and browsed therein by night; and We were witnesses to their judgement. We made Sulaymān to understand [the case]; and unto each of them We gave judgement and knowledge.' (21:78-9) The two Prophets, upon them be peace, had given different *fatwās*; and Sulaymān's was the more correct, but as Prophets they were infallible (*maᶜṣūm*), and hence Daūd's judgement was acceptable also.

Understanding this is the key to recreating the spirit of tolerance among Muslims. Shaykh Ömer Bilmen summarises the jurists' position as follows: 'The fundamentals of the religion, namely basic doctrine, the obligatory status of the forms of worship, and the ethical virtues, are the subject of universal agreement, an agreement to which everyone is religiously obliged to subscribe. Those who diverge from the rulings accepted by the overwhelming majority of ordinary Muslims are considered to be the people of *bidᶜa* and misguidance, since the *dalīls* (proof-texts) establishing them are clear. But it is not a violation of any Islamic obligation for differences of opinion to exist concerning the *furūᶜ* (branches) and *juz'iyyāt* (secondary issues) which devolve from these basic principles. In fact, such differences are a necessary expression of the Divine wisdom.' (Bilmen, I, 329.)

A further point needs elucidating. If the jurists may legitimately disagree, how should the Islamic state apply a unified legal code throughout its territories? Clearly, the law must be the same everywhere. Imām al-Qarāfī states the answer clearly: 'The head of state gives a judgement concerning the [variant rulings which have been reached by] *ijtihād*, and this does away with the disagreement, and obliges those who follow *ijtihād* verdicts which conflict with the head of state's to adopt his verdict.' (Qarāfī, II, 103; affirmed also in Āmidī, IV, 273-4.) Obviously this is a counsel specifically for *qāḍīs*, and applies only to questions of public law, not to rulings on worship.

70 This was understood as early as the 18th century. Al-Būṭī quotes Shāh Walīullāh al-Dahlawī (*Ḥujjat Allāh al-Bāligha*, I, 132) as observing: 'The Umma up to the present date ... has unanimously agreed that these four recorded *madhhabs* may be followed by way of taqlīd. In this there are manifest benefits and advantages, especially in these days in which enthusiasm has dimmed greatly, and souls have been given to drink of their own passions, so that everyone with an opinion is delighted with his opinion.' This reminds us that Islam is not a totalitarian religion which denies the possibility and legitimacy of variant opinions. 'The Muslim scholars are agreed that the *mujtahid* cannot incur a sin in regard to his legitimate *ijtihād* exercised to derive judgements of *Sharīᶜa*. [Only the likes of] Bishr al-Marīsī, Ibn ᶜAliyya, Abū Bakr al-Aṣamm and the deniers of *qiyās*, such as the Muᶜtazilites and the Twelver Shīᶜa, believe that there is only one true ruling in each legal issue, so that whoever does not attain to it is a sinner.' (Āmidī, IV, 244.) This is of course an aspect of the Divine mercy, and a token of the sane and generous breadth of Islam. 'Allah desires ease for you, not difficulty.' (Koran, 2:185) 'I am sent to make things easy, not to make them more difficult.' (Bukhārī, ᶜIlm, 12.) 'Never was Allah's Messenger, may blessings and pease be upon him, given the choice between two options but that he chose the easier of them, unless it was a sin.' (Bukhārī, Manāqib, 23.) But the process lamented in Dahlawī's day, by which people simply ignored this Sunna principle, has nowadays become far more poisonous. What is particularly damaging is that egos have become so powerful that the old Muslim *adab* of polite tolerance during debate has been lost in some circles, as people find it hard to accept that other Muslims might hold opinions that differ from their own. It must be realised that if Allah tells Mūsā (upon him be peace) to speak 'gently' to Pharoah (20:43), and commands us 'not to debate with the People of the Book save in a most excellent way,' (29:46) then how much more important must it be to debate politely with people who are neither Pharoahs nor Christians, but are of our own religion?

71 Probably because of an underlying insecurity, many young Muslim activists cannot bear to admit that they might not know something about their religion. And this despite

the example of Imām Mālik, who, when asked forty questions about *fiqh*, answered 'I do not know' (*lā adrī*) to thirty-six of them. (Āmidī, IV, 221; Bilmen, I, 249.) How many egos nowadays can bear to admit ignorance even once? They should remember the saying: 'He who makes most haste to give a *fatwā*, makes most haste to the Fire.' (Bilmen, I, 255.) Imām al-Subkī condemns 'those who make haste to give *fatwās*, relying on the apparent meaning of the [revealed] phrases without thinking deeply about them, thereby dragging other people into ignorance, and themselves into the agonies of Hell.' (Tāj al-Dīn al-Subkī, *Muʿīd al-Niʿam wa-Mubīd al-Niqam* (Brill, 1908), 149. Even Imām al-Shaʿbī (d. 103), out of his modesty and *adab*, and his awareness of the great complexity of the *fiqh*, did not consider himself a *muftī*, only a *nāqil* (transmitter of texts). (Bilmen, I, 256.)

72 Cf. Imām al-Dajawī, II, 579: 'By Allah, this view (that ordinary people should not follow *madhhabs*) is nothing less than an attempt to fling the door wide open for people's individual preferences, thereby turning the Book and the Sunna into playthings to be manipulated by those deluded fools, driven by their compounded ignorance and their corrupt imaginings. It is obvious that personal preferences vary enormously, and that ignorant people will arrive at their conclusions on the basis of their own emotions and imaginings. So what will be the result if we put them in authority over the *Sharīʿa*, so that they are able to interpret it in the light of their own opinions, and play with it according to their own preferences?'

73 Būṭī, 107-8. The same image is used by Imran Nyazee: '*Taqlīd*, as distinguished from blind conservatism, is the foundation of all relationships based on trust, like those between a patient and his doctor, a client and his lawyer, and a business and its accountant. It is a legal method for ensuring that judges who are not fully-qualified *mujtahids* may be able to decide cases in the light of precedents laid down by independent jurists ... The system of *taqlīd* implies that as long as the layman does not get the training for becoming a doctor he cannot practice medicine, for example. In the case of medicine such a person may be termed a quack and may even be punished today, but in the case of Islamic law he is assuming a much graver responsibility: he is claiming that the opinion he is expressing is the law intended by Allah.' (Introduction to *The Distinguished Jurist's Primer*, xxxv.)

74 It hardly needs adding, as a final observation, that nothing in all the above should be understood as an objection to the extension and development of the *fiqh* in response to modern conditions. Much serious *ijtihād* is urgently called for; the point being made in this paper is simply that such *ijtihād* must be carried out only by scholars fully qualified to do so.